T0083548

MANATEE
LAGOON

MANATEE LAGOON

poems

Jenna Le

ACRE
CINCINNATI 2022

Acre Books is made possible by the support of the
Robert and Adele Schiff Foundation and the Department
of English at the University of Cincinnati.

ISBN-13 (pbk) 978-1-946724-51-9
ISBN-13 (ebook) 978-1-946724-52-6

Designed by Barbara Neely Bourgoyne
Cover art: photo by George Potter, via Unsplash

The press is based at the University of Cincinnati, Department of English
and Comparative Literature, McMicken Hall, Room 248, PO Box 210069,
Cincinnati, OH, 45221-0069.

Acre Books books may be purchased at a discount for educational use.
For information please email business@acre-books.com.

CONTENTS

YELLOWED WEEDS DERANGED

THE FAIRY TALE NOW FINISHED

I SING: HOLY

THE MOTHER OF MERMAIDS

WHAT THE ANCIENT GREEK SAILORS KNEW

When you're nutritionally imbalanced,
too many sodium ions in your blood
or too few of potassium, so that the salt-fringed air
coaxes music out of your vitamin deficiencies
like calliope pipes, and you tremble invisibly
like a locus on the airwaves between two radio stations,
two opposed political pundits flickering in and out
of audible range as a semitruck winds down the interstate
in the wee hours, the sickly milk sky uncertain
as to whether it is dawn or delirium, the trucker
himself uncertain as to whether he is in Illinois or Indiana
or merely dreaming,
and at any moment you might be on the verge
of zigzagging out of personhood and not know it
because there is no line of chalk—only dolphins—
then it happens. It's happening right now. You're becoming
a plaything of raw neurons, and the starlight
is squashing your brain's synapses flat with its baby thumbs,
and you are surrendering to it
because there is nowhere else to go. When this happens
to elderly patients in hospitals, doctors call it *sundowning*,
a name implying that when the sun rises,
everything will be normal again,
but you are not elderly, you are thirty, which in ancient Greece
might mean you are two-thirds done with your life
and anyway you are not in a hospital
but out to sea, a place everyone knows
doesn't really exist, where creatures that don't exist called *sea horses*
are sometimes thrown by the waves on the wood
at your feet, and other creatures called *manatees*
with sideways teats tell you with their sad huge eyes
they could love you like no land wife ever could.

WHAT DO YOU WANT TO BE WHEN YOU GROW UP?

As an imaginative kid who loved to read about the myth of mermaids,
I wanted not to be a doctor or a writer but a mother of mermaids.

I'd heard that if I swallowed whole the tough, translucent tails of shrimp,
they'd somehow find their way into my uterus and I'd give birth to mermaids.

I'd hoard shrimp tails inside a napkin, pop them one by one in secret,
then scan my pee with greedy eyes to see if in it slithered mermaids.

Some kids incline toward witch-and-warlock lore. I was too chickenshit.
Some kids are drawn to vampires, some to werewolves. Me, I would just rather
    mermaids.

An insecure young girl, I craved the praise of supermarket strangers;
I wanted them to gawk: "There goes the goddess in whose belly gather mermaids!"

And, like my mom, I longed to parent special kids who could achieve
what I could not, swim places barred to me. Therefore, I staked my worth on
    mermaids.

ECHOES

To me, who grew up in the 1980s,
the 1980s were a foreign planet.
Besides the sounds of vacuuming that daily
sent angry tremors through our walls, volcanic
shudders that nudged my cagey nerves to panic
(I sensed the wrath their rattling indicated),
the soundtrack of my youth was pomegranate-
strange: a fruitcake dateless and outdated.

Driving me to and from my math-team practice,
Dad played cassette tapes featuring the voices
of '60s Saigon divas, the twittering accents
of Thái Thanh and Khánh Ly, the lung-full noises
of bosomy laments for soldier boys
sent off to war, to butcher and be hacked at,
and odes for stout-waist matriarchs who hoisted
sick infants on their backs, dry-cheeked as cactus.

Mom's music tastes were more diverse: LPs
of old-time country singers, Emmylou
and Crystal Gayle; ABBA, the '70s
brash beach-blond Bobbsey twins; the ingenues
of France's yé-yé period, who crooned
American songs rendered awkwardly
in French as if they owned those borrowed tunes,
big-haired Sylvie Vartan and Françoise Hardy.

We watched few movies, and the few we did
were Taiwanese, dubbed in Vietnamese:
mixed-race Fei Xiang in polo shirt amid
his stringy bandmates, strumming to appease
his wayward lover Idy Chan; or, seized

by girlish mischievousness, Brigitte Lin
slinkily sneaking up behind Han Chin
to shove him off his rock into the reeds.

Then, too, the hokey choreography
of *Paris by Night*, undying vaudeville show
adored by every Viet war refugee
though no one non-Viet ever seems to know
what we are blabbering about when we
effuse about the costumes, the marquees,
the saucy grins of singers Tommy Ngô
and Lynda Trang Đài (who, these days, sells pho).

SIBLING RIVALRY

Besides the dead one, there were two of us,
both girls. Our family was small compared
to, say, the March clan based at Orchard House
or the Bennets of Longbourn, but we shared
an outsize sense of our own worth: like fractals,
our finite brains housed infinite ambition.
One winter, on a blood-red rug, we acted
out *Little Women*: with panache and passion
I played the part of Jo, while my sister brought
her taller height to bear on the role of Bhaer.
We made believe that we were lovers, fought
with dog-wet tongues in the playroom's dry, hot air
to find out who would dominate, who'd win
this war of words we'd both been drafted in.

A VERY ASIAN VARIATION

I used to think that part of being Asian
was not owning a dishwasher: Dad
standing at the sink, his scouring pad
bringing the fight to contamination,
more tough and thorough at elimination
of grit and grease than any man or lad
born on US soil that I've ever had
the chance to test. Upon my relocation
to an apartment in whose kitchen stood
one of those mythic suds machines, I worried
I'd somehow lost some of my Asian blood.
That night, I watched my worry dissipate
when, as I loaded the machine, my curried
chopsticks kept falling through the bottom grate.

BIRD

We heard her   and came running

We heard her

wings blurred

We heard her   fly up the metal chute

only to find herself

                          self-entrapped in our laundry room

                          self-buried in our linen hoard

her exit route barred

We heard her   throat burr

We heard her

wings blurred   so we came running

                          feet bare on the red-carpeted stairs

We heard her   so we herded her

We harried her

                          toward an opened window, a soft sunlit square

amid the hard boards

We hurried her   and harried her

and herded her

                                 toward the open air

our broom-waving horde   must have seemed to her a horror

for all that we   heralded   her liberty

ON THE LESSER-KNOWN USES OF MEAT TENDERIZER

Once I began to menstruate at thirteen,
I rapidly became an expert at
expunging bloodstains from pajamas, jeans,
dresses, bedsheets, upholstery, even mats
and rugs. I'm ready for a life of crime
now, armed with skills ideally suited for
a career of carving finger-deep red lines
in victims' throats, disposing of their cars
in forested ravines. You need to learn
the art of covering your tracks before
making tracks, you must master how to burn
love letters prior to allowing your
mind to love, and you must know how to strike
the backspace key before you learn to write.

PRIVATE RITUALS

I edit my posts not so much for content
but because I loathe the lowercase *f*

—how uncouth it looks! how asymmetric,
top-heavy and out of balance,

as if at any moment its skewed bouffant
might topple it toward the right margin,

its top curl looking for all the world
like a stray pubic hair

that sticks out past the neat straight hem
of its outvoted crossbar

—and so I wrinkle my nose at words
like *of*, *off*, *if*, and *distaff*,

words so lacking in God's good sense
that they give pride of place to a whore

like the letter *f*, and if I'm forced
to use such almost-blasphemous words,

as, being an English speaker, I despondently
daily must,

then I hide them in the shadow of words
that end with the righteous letter *d*

like this:

.....................................if
...............................mind

...................................half
...................................mad

—see how much better that feels? and can you fathom
you're the first soul I've told

PURSES

in mem. Kate Spade

When our Quiz Bowl team of eighteen-year-olds snagged
        a berth in the finals, held in New York City,

        my small-town Minnesotan brain cells dizzied—
at last I'd be some place that *mattered*. Swag

was my teammate Anne's fixation: knockoff bags
        peddled in Chinatown, affixed with glitzy

        Kate Spade labels. Anne bought a sack of six,
then forgot it on the airport shuttle's shag

seats; someone swiped it within minutes. Kate,
        I learned a fact of womanhood that year:

even we knockoff girls, cheap, desperate
to look like someone else, to imitate

        a finer woman, have our value; we're
        wanted, wanted, until we disappear.

LOSING MYSELF
IN ART

NEUROLOGY WARD SKETCHBOOK

Every 250 feet, I spy
a shiny placard pasted on the wall
to tell the convalescents tottering by
how far they've walked so far, and give them all
encouragement to slog a little more
each day than they had slogged the day before.

I pace a dozen laps around this jail,
so fiercely that the aide whose black cloth mask
is blazoned with an orange swallowtail
dubs me a "model patient"; then I sink back
against my bed and drag my sketchbook out.
The nurses, both the lithe ones and the stout,

so quickly flutter round the nursing station,
my pencil can't keep up with their blurred shapes.
The neurosurgeons, rounding on their patients
in brusque, brisk-shuffling clogs, likewise escape
me. Only the neurologists, who lumber
like manatees, get limned in gray and umber.

PATTI SMITH, 1976

This photo, black-and-white, where Mapplethorpe
portrays his dark-mopped ex in profile, seated
nude on wooden floorboards, knees drawn up
against her breasts to hide her nipples, heated
by the sideways radiator pipes
on which she rests her palms, her bulging ribs
a set of parallel oblique gray stripes
rippling her bare white skin, unsmiling lips
a short flat line—
                        these were my first parameters,
my inspirations, when I learned to write.
On Patti's ribs, the wooden flooring's planks,
the stacked pale pipes, I modeled my pentameters.
The aim: amid such sharp lines, to be frank
and raw, yet still control what sees the light.

DEIPNOSOPHISTAE

Come visit my new place
and see the novelties
I use to decorate:
my ornamental plates,
my tall black-figure vase,
my souvenirs from Greece,
the map of the Peloponnese
I've tacked above my bed.
Its inlets and its bays
make me feel at peace.
With it hanging overhead,
I sleep sounder than the dead.
Think you can prove me wrong?
Please go ahead! Go on!
Please visit at your ease,
any night you please.
I have such nice belongings
I wish that you could see.
I even have the book
where Athenaeus relates
how the loveliest girl in Greece
once laid Diogenes,
the homely sage, for free.

TO JOHN ASHBERY

Twenty-two, awkward as a mittened hand,
cheeks always blushing as if red with cold,
I'd lately bumbled to New York, enrolled
in school. Unlike the immigrant who manned
the char-blacked, spicy-smoked halal food stand
I lunched at daily or the squelchy-soled
madame whose mops kept dorm floors free of mold,
I brought no useful skills to my new land
—no assets but my youth, and I, small hipped,
flat chested, did not have, unlike some youths,
the sort of youth that can be swapped for brass.
While merciless schoolmasters drilled my class
on heeding hierarchy, staying on script,
you taught me meaning lies down twistier routes.

THE BALLAD OF GREAT-UNCLE CHỈ

for Bửu Chỉ (1948–2002)

Great-Uncle Chi, an artist jailed
for protesting the war,
made many ink-on-paper drawings
while living behind bars.

His drawings show gaunt hangdog men,
feet buried in packed snow,
who moonward reach with outspread hands
as though hefting a canoe.

His drawings show sopping-hearted men
with cacti where their hands
should be. They show vermin wielding scepters
above a melted land.

They show starved men whose biceps shrank
to the size of turkey wattles.
They show men doubled over, faces
blank as empty bottles.

They show brothers sparring to the death
who yesterday were born.
The moon above them's black: a chewed-up,
spat-out peppercorn.

Chi's art was smuggled overseas
by friends from his school days,
poets who met in broken-paned pubs
to talk their pain away.

"Remember how Chi used to paint
nudes in the old French style?
What ample flesh those beauties had!
What pink cheeks! What moon-white smiles!"

POSTURE

after *Le Viol* by Edgar Degas

I knew a man with posture just like this—
loafers spread wide apart, hands casually
shoved in pants pockets, leaning at his ease
against a door. As if he owned the place.
He was my med-school classmate. Unafraid
of sickness, death, his patients, or his bosses,
he'd stand with this relaxed and cocky posture
among the ICU's tube-tangled beds
and rattle off the latest blood-test findings
in a loud, bored voice. One irked attending
commented, "A guy who stands like that
is bound to be a surgeon." Maybe not bad,
but careless. When a patient's health got worse
from a mistake he made, he blamed a nurse.

WOMAN BEHIND THE LENS

Quarried in Italy, hewn in America,
cosseted by San Francisco, uncorseted by Hollywood,
widowed by smallpox, remarried in Mexico,
comrade of Pablo, paramour of Diego, betrayer of Frida,
documentarian of the starkly colored murals of José Clemente
with their ruthless turbines and lurid vivisections,
photographer of farmhands and unionists,
of women with speckled brown pendulous breasts
and babies with hair as soft and hot as the fine snow
flicked from a cigarette,

muse of the Mexican Communist Party,
target of Italy's fascist police,
suspect in two assassinations,
smeared by state-run newspapers as a tiger-clawed *pistolera*,
detained, interrogated, exiled, and finally eliminated,
Tina Modotti,
a seamstress's daughter,
renounced photography at thirty-five:
"I can't solve life's problems by losing
myself in art's."

WOMEN WHO CONJURE OWLS

1

They peeled her newborn from the slick of sweat
that sheened the light-tan insides of her arms
and sent her a thousand miles away to fret

the next three years inside a locked, alarm-
rigged TB hospital. The baby was given
up for adoption; later, she was informed

by nasal voices that her elder children
died of disease while she was quarantined.
Riding on Mother Owl depicts a coven

of birds with human eyes, a gravel-skinned
owl-matriarch, two coal-red hatchlings balanced
upon her shoulders, coasting on the wind

so effortlessly that her spread black talons
seem to be standing still on soundless snow.

2

Today is Easter Sunday. I sit reading
web articles about the Inuit
workshops at Kinngait. Many of their leading

artists are women, thumb-webs gray with grit
as they etch copper blocks with nitric acid,
or chisel shadows into stone, or treat

smooth lithographic plates with sticky wax.
Kenojuak Ashevak's dad, I learn, was killed
when she was scarcely six, caught in a clash

between those like himself who knew the skill
of channeling the spirits and those who
adhered to Christian tenets. In Oakville,

the stained-glass window she designed: an owl
feeds multitudes with one shared fish, ice-blue.

3

In *Following the Route*, an oversize
owl, black plumes specked with small white dots,
looks straight ahead with goatlike oblong eyes

fixed on his bourn. He oars a dark-blue boat,
his only passenger a frowning seal.
Nikotai Mills, I think I know the route

he's following, this ramrod-postured owl
who doesn't need to fly to get to where
he's going and who graciously takes fares.

But teach me what ecstatic notes unspool
from the accordion held by the fat
white owl with massive biceps who sits square

athwart your print *Bird Song*. Why does he play,
not sing? Why's his accordion red—with what?

VENUS FRIGIDA

Sine Cerere et Baccho friget Venus.
—TERENCE

The Frozen Venus is the image caption,
a homage to the jaundiced Latin maxim,
"All love grows cold when food and drink are absent."

Depicted in a sickly green-lit landscape,
the fair-flanked goddess squats on balled red fabric
and hugs her wind-nipped trunk to fend off gangrene

from frostbite, while her son emits a rattly
cough in the vicinity of her waxen
knees. She pointedly ignores a goat-eared man-beast,

an umber muscled satyr, hovering blackly
mere inches from the pair, a bulging basket
on his arm—I don't buy it for a fraction

of a second. I've been cold before. If Madam
Venus were really cold, she'd grab that damask
beneath her hock and wrap it round her fat-knobbed

back. I've been cold. If I were in this tableau,
I'd grab pale Cupid, press him to my mammaries,
absorbing all his heat. Good Lord, I'd gladly

tackle the brown goat man himself and wrassle
him to the dirt. That Terence was a hack:
if love were great enough, it'd conquer. Come back.

GOLDEN SHOVEL IN THE VOICE OF MARGOT BEGEMANN

I crumple marriage offers made by fishermen,
masons, bakers of brioche, for I know
my consecration is to marry the
great van Gogh. Look at history and see
men of genius wrecked before there is
the chance for one brave girl to swoop down, dangerous
to his enemies and doubters, the
critics and hecklers, and save him from that storm.
My love shall be his shield, prevent the terrible.

No shy virgin, I've seen four decades; they
have handled me the way some clumsy half-
cocked violin restorer does a never-
again-same harp. I know the score. I found
Vincent living with his mother in these
snake-filled backwoods, where gossips embroider the dangers
of his past romancing of a whore. Sufficient
to say I'm not scared off. Inside me, too,
there is a prostitute and a barkeep,
a seamstress and a siren and a shore.

YELLOWED WEEDS
DERANGED

SIRENIAN SERMON

in response to a January 2021 news item reporting a Florida manatee
had been found with a presidential candidate's name etched in its back

A manatee is no cartouche.
A manatee is not a blimp.
No pharaoh's name or Nike swoosh
carved in her flanks shall ever crimp

her honey-languid swimming strokes.
She is no singing telegram,
no contrail, and no ad for smokes.
The same way you would treat the lamb,

thus you shall treat the manatee,
whose every breath's a stinky huff,
who shuffles upstream clownishly.
Love's not just for the pretty stuff,

a fact I thought you'd understand.
Man's what he is, yet God loved man.

THE MORNING AFTER THE ELECTION

The morning after the election, we
converge, as usual, on the bus stop: three
commuters with no commonality
except our silent shared dependency

on public transportation. I don't know
the other two commuters' names, although
each day for weeks we've stood here in a row,
craning our necks to watch the bus's slow

climb up the skinny frog-cold, fog-wet lane.
Overnight, something in the air has changed:
the gusts that leave the yellowed weeds deranged
now make us tremble for an unexplained

split second longer than before. The square-
backed woman in black wool stands just a hair
more near to me than previously, to share
warmth. I smile shyly, prompting her to bare

a crescent of white teeth, though her black eyes
in her black face stay somber. To my right,
the other bus-stop regular, a light-
skinned girl with wiry spectacles and tight

glossy curls, ventures, voice soft as velour:
"You ladies think it's gonna snow?" "Not sure,"
I answer. We discuss the temperature;
the curly girl is scared she can't endure

New Hampshire's famed harsh snows: until July,
she lived in Georgia. "Moved for work," she sighs.

I give my name; "I'm Sahja," she replies.
A surge of fellow feeling warms the sky

around us three, a fragile tender flutter.
In this new world, we must protect each other.

GUSANOZ

We leave for good. I-89
absorbs my little Honda Civic
into its southbound lane. Quick
it's not: most times, we're plovers flying
when we take this road (in north
New Hampshire, traffic is a rarity),
but luggage wedged into the narrow
gap between the third and fourth
snow tires in the trunk weighs down
the car so that we're trudging syrup,
and making turns is actual work.
My blood flows light, however, stirred
by hope: I'm moving to New York.
It'll all work out when we reach town.

It'll all work out when we reach town:
a chorus of champagne flutes' clinks
awaits. No more will we be jinxed
by clock hands spinning, spinning round.
Fresh start. Sure, there are things I'll miss
about New England, like that weekend
at Stowe, the bath steam, snowmelt leaking
from ski boots in the corner. Bliss.
Still, it's pleasant to return
where spicy restaurants are plenty:
the only spot where you could sate
a taco lust near my old place
was Gusanoz, their always friendly
staff warning, "Careful—you'll get burned!"

Their staff warned, "Careful—you'll get burned!"
How long ago was that? An age?
This morning, an ex-colleague's rage

on Twitter caught my eye: his stern
avatar scowled above a pic
he'd scanned in from the *Valley News*
where, under halcyon heaven's blues,
a line of orange cones inflicts
a gash upon the highway. "Border
Patrol checkpoint on Interstate
89 snarls traffic, stirs strife,"
the headline reads. The piece relates
Gusanoz's busboy's been deported.
His boss: "Great kid. . . . They've ruined his life."

His boss: "Great kid. . . . They've ruined his life."
Gulping the article, I burn,
for all that I'd been warned. I learn
eleven folks were seized by ICE.
An agent who wouldn't show his badge
threatened the neighbors who, concerned,
approached the scene, a clash that spurred
one woman's fretting, "Will six large
men with dogs stop me with no warrant?"
Border Patrol? We're near no coast,
this inland town with tourist charms.
Last fall, my sister and I threaded
through a corn maze owned by a redhead
who was most kind, the perfect host.

The farmers here are kind, good hosts.
So what has happened to this place
I lived until last week, this space
amid the mountains where my most
fulfilling job was teaching all
who came from all around the earth

to learn? Will these kids now get hurt?
I shot a text out to my pal
who lives up north still. She replied
to say she has begun to carry
her green card in her wallet, wary.
And when she used her car to ferry
our mutual friend to class, he smiled
but gripped his passport the whole ride.

He gripped his passport the whole ride—
and here I'm talking big brave guys,
ceiling-tall, enormous smiles,
the type that's eager to provide
pointers to more junior learners.
The news has got them worried. All
of us are worried. I, now walled
in the Big Apple, am a furnace
of worry. That stern prof on Twitter
scowls, pounds on "Block" and on "Ignore."
This rural town, to be quite clear,
is miles and miles from the perimeter.
There's just one sandwich counter here:
Cambodian. Nice town, like yours;

and combed by Border Patrol, like yours
has two-thirds odds of being, Reader.
You thought the edge was far, yet teeter.
Lay Yi, her birthplace mined by wars,
migrated in 2004
and now she's feeding hungry locals
at this sandwich joint, a focal
point in the neighborhood, a core.
She greets me by my name each time.

When moving out, I went to say
goodbye, but she was out that day.
Perhaps it's fitting: farewells could
give the sense one leaves for good
when one drives down I-89.

BIRD-WATCHING IN THE AFTERMATH

speaking of snowy owls I
want you to know only
the male of the species
is white the female is
mixed and some say
less beautiful

a related fact
is all *Bubo scandiacus*
have yellow eyes
and yet Pinterest
is cluttered
with doctored photos
of snowy owls
with blue eyes   why
because a white
creature with blue
eyes is considered so
desirable that
if it doesn't exist
people will twist
themselves into knots
to make it exist
using Photoshop to swap
yellows for blues
the ultimate innocent
little white lie

but the human brain tells other
lies too and the spinal cord
white on its surface
gray at its core makes even
worse decisions we

call them knee-jerk reflexes
and rightly condemn them
but when we look in the mirror
we should be looking
at more than our knees

QUIXOTIC

Plymouth, New Hampshire

We shrieked *Eyesore!*, blew raspberries, chagrined
when Groton's turbines loomed on the horizon
in the most literal sense. No charming wind-
mills of the Old Dutch waffle-wingèd kind,
these power generators, gray-shark-finned,
are starkly functional as streptomycin
and rawboned as a weasel that's been skinned.
They crimp the mountain range whose shade we rise in

each sunup, snarl its formerly streamlined
shape into one that there's no recognizing.
Their sharp Inquisitorial blades remind
us we're the sinning scions of folks who sinned
in their own times. We're told these shineless tined
machines are meant to save us from a poison
we fed ourselves, deluged our unrefined
intestines with. What starchy moralizing.

DISPATCH FROM HANOVER, NEW HAMPSHIRE

1

Mid-February's here. *The president*
inaugurated three short weeks ago
just turned the EPA's reins over to
a climate-change denier, Salon laments.

Today's high: 49 degrees. Ice sculptures
across the Dartmouth Green are melting fast,
limbs snapping off and shattering. Funny that
when temps start rising, ice gets cloudy-colored

as if it thinks, like some postmodern writers,
opaqueness has the power to thwart extinction.
Just yesterday, upon this chiseled gryphon's
outstretched right paw, there perched an owl of ice.

2

At three years old, I had a vivid nightmare:
my mom was standing at her bedroom window,
lifting the gauzy curtain with one hand so
she could see. The lamp cast golden light where

she lingered on that crisp midwinter evening,
excitedly calling me to come and look:
"You won't believe this! Right here on our block—
a big ice sculpture! A miracle, all gleaming

beneath the Boughtons' porch lights. . . ." Rapt, she stared.
But I was mad at her—some childish snit—
and feigned I did not hear her. Dragged my feet.
When I relented, there was nothing there.

CAPGRAS/SEAGRASS

You sometimes think you suffer from Capgras.

Sea turtles, without thinking too much about it, feed on seagrass.

Capgras syndrome is a psychiatric condition wherein the afflicted cannot be dissuaded from the horror-inducing belief that her friends and family are, in fact, impostors wearing close-fitting skin suits and uncannily lifelike human masks.

Seagrass is a vegetation common to shore-adjacent marine environments, the sustenance of not only sea turtles but also manatees and even some fish such as mullet.

Whose eyes are those, looking out of your mother's face? Whose face is that, snugly encircling your mother's eyes, like the setting of two counterfeit gemstones?

As quantities of seagrass dwindle due to unchecked real-estate development, pollution, and other human factors, ocean ecosystems are being upturned, their centers ripped out, like a face without eyes.

Still, the nature documentary ends on a note of cautious optimism: if only we can motivate ourselves to enact sensible policies such as turning one-third of the world's oceans into protected reserves, populations of threatened species such as sea turtles will bounce back.

Tonight, in the effusively golden, deceptively warm light of your TV room lamp, you thought your boyfriend of six years looked not at all like himself, but like his younger self gussied up to look like his older self, and this made you feel not horror but tenderness.

HOW I KNOW IMPLICIT BIAS EXISTS

Turn right on Mascoma, left on Glen, left on Main, left on Interchange.
I recited this like a nursery rhyme until I knew it by heart.
Then, to be extra sure I wouldn't mess up, I also punched the destination
into my GPS, turned the volume up loud.

I went off course within minutes. Despite my GPS, despite my angelic
intentions. I had cut my teeth driving the right-
angled blocks of Manhattan, but the intersections here were shaped like
scalenes, buckyballs, Emily Dickinson's envelope poems.

When the GPS shrilled, "Turn left!" I turned left, but not far enough left,
and I lost the election. Just kidding. I didn't lose the election, but I lost
all sense of where I was. Got sucked into the suicide-spiral-
that-should-have-been-a-rotary outside the scrappy Cambodian

sandwich shop. Cars piled up behind me as I slowed to figure out
where the hell I was. Not wanting the other drivers to groan, "That awful
Asian woman driver!" I picked up my pace, figuring that
not confirming people's stereotypes was more important

than getting where I needed to go. When I got to forks in the road,
I made decisions at random. Quick was more important than correct.
The GPS kept shrilling, but it sounded
like a foreign language now. "Take High Street!" it twittered,

but there was no High Street in sight. "In eight hundred feet, make a U-turn,"
it begged, but I didn't want to die. Yesterday I taught a class
of high-school students. The topic was women writers. After I got home
I realized I had talked about two male writers I liked and somehow forgot

to mention any women writers at all. You think I'm joking,
but I have always prided myself on being a feminist. Yet there I had stood
in front of these kids, unconsciously
calling on boys more often than girls. I never found the Interchange.

PLEASE DON'T TELL ME HOW THE STORY ENDS

A Vermont man. Rural. Lacerated
his knee with a chainsaw
doing tree work one summer.
The wound festered, not angrily
but with a slow simmering
puzzlement. This lasted years.
One day he fingered it, felt
something hard inside, pulled
out a shiny piece of glass.
Another time, he pulled a blade
of grass out of it, then
a whole maple leaf, so perfect
it filled Canadian flag makers with envy.
Started feeling mighty proud of himself,
like King Arthur when he made that stone
belch up a sword. Began pulling
bigger and bigger things
out of his knee: a dime,
a dollar bill, a bandanna,
a quail's egg. And the quail hatched, too.
Got to calling himself The Wizard,
made the circuit of local festivals,
state fairs. You'd think this story ends
some place bad—a psych ward,
OR, or early grave—a wimpled lady
shoveling dirt on a corpse
that died of three parts delusion,
one part gangrene. But I think
the times have just gotten to you,
the pessimists opining on TV
have dragged you down to their level.
The Vermonter, he's still
making the rounds, still finding

7-Eleven receipts, perfectly folded
road maps, and poetry broadsheets
tied with slim blue ribbons
in his knee. Sometimes butterflies
come foaming out, five or six at once,
beating lavender wings.

TO A PHYSICIAN KILLED BY GUN VIOLENCE

You climbed the stairs to middle age
and just beyond, your footsteps trained
to make no creaking noise, your veined
hand mute upon the balustrade

so that your snoring spouse, his cage
of matted hair propped on a doubled
plinth of pillows, could sleep untroubled,
your daughter with her snaking braid

doze undisturbed when you returned
from work. You wore your own hair short,
like shadow—nothing here to court
notice, to creak or squeak or glint

or gleam. Those seeing you discerned
no youth, no unformed possibility;
they only saw someone who willingly
did the work until she didn't.

THE ORIGAMI MASTER BREAKFASTS WITH HIS NEW APPRENTICE

This gentle wind: it'll blow away
a dry napkin but not a wet one.
Still, my origami beasts
aren't safe, must be moved
off the window ledge.

Observe this one right here:
neither crane nor cicada.
None of that traditional stuff for me! Not now.
This century, this dynasty,
this outlandishly wigged king,

they call for
new strategies, modern weaponry,
exotic species.
This one I'm holding in my palms
was modeled after a strange fish

my lover saw from his ship
sailing back from Australia,
a wrinkled warm-blooded codger
(no, I'm not
talking of my lover now, impertinent child).

It looks shapeless to you, I know:
scarcely recognizable
as one of God's creatures.
But, as with sunlight,
your eyes will grow used to its face

in a blink or two.
Then you'll be able

to see nothing else,
not even with your eyes shut.
It's like that with me now:

when my eyelids touch, I always smell
the sea. . . .
I wish I'd been there with him
the first time
he saw this bizarre organism,

its pudgy snout, dimpled chin, short
arms, stiff tapered tail.
Though it dwarfed
his largest horse by half,
he wasn't scared, not for a second.

You see, exotic
doesn't always mean dangerous.
(He said that to me too, the night we met.
It was at a tavern by the docks,
where the foreign merchant ships anchor.)

I think I'll teach you
how to fold this one
today, once the dishes are cleared.
It's an easy one to start with,
it will teach your hands confidence.

You'll need that lesson
in coming days. This century, this dynasty. . . .
When the dugong splashed him,
he staggered. Brine clung to his nose hairs,
stinging. Then it lightly swam away.

THE FAIRY TALE
NOW FINISHED

THE TWELVE DANCING PRINCESSES

The fairy tale now finished, the fusilier
mulls: should he marry sixteen-year-old Lina,
the spunky youngest sister, the minx whose ear
was sharp enough to hear the harmed larch keen, or

should he wed the eldest, Thérèse, aged twenty-nine,
the stern-browed martinet who barked out orders
at her ditzy sisters, keeping them in line
as their rowboats nosed toward Fae-Land's reedy borders?

There are two versions of this old French legend:
in the first version, the romantic one
that charmed me as a child who got piled on

for being the smallest, the soldier smiles and says,
"I choose cherubic Lina," while in the second,
my favorite now, he smirks, "Give me Thérèse."

THE READER

"Don't date a lot of boys. It's better far to marry
your first love, like I did," the gray-haired woman said.
The teen girl scoffed at this advice; she longed to carry

out what she thought to be a full life, rich with varied
experience, like in the novels she had read.
And so she dated many boys and did not marry

at all, and sad guitarists sang her wild unwary
heart, her tangled hair, her hot impulsive head.
The girl basked in their singing and went on to carry

on love affairs whose bitterness was legendary,
that ended in glass shards and horse heads left in beds.
And when she'd had her fill, she thought at last she'd marry,

for wedded life and childbirth, too, have literary
worth, featuring in many novels' central threads.
And so she found a husband who was proud to carry

into their house his bride whose interplanetary
picaresque past just proved she'd tried and risked and bled.
They raised a girl and boy. And they stayed happily married.
She never spoke of that one throbbing scar she carried.

NEW YORK LIVING

My upstairs neighbor
puffs cigarettes
on the fire escape
post-porn-viewing. Lets

the flaccid butts
rain from his hand
so that they pile up
on the first-floor landing

where my downstairs neighbor
has installed a quaint
tub of carnations.
She is no saint

herself, plays horrid
music at bizarre
hours so that my floor
shakes with sitar

wails ad nauseam.
Vacuums her rugs
at six a.m.
when I still lie snug

in bed and nodding.
Sandwiched between
these two dark gods,
these powers unseen,

the one above
whose hand rains fire
and the one below
with her shrieking choirs,

I think about
how my childhood books
split north and south
between seraphs and spooks,

hell's dread torments
and heaven's bright qualities.
I must invent
a new theology.

A FAILED GEORGIC

A fellow poet challenges my ass
to write a "georgic": verse lines that grandstand
by telling readers how to use the land.

I've never owned land. Not one gob of grass!
Monthly, I make a stinky stack of cash
and fork it to some fakely smiling man
so that the cops won't clap me in the can
for squatting on a scuffed linoleum patch
that sits on concrete stilts above another
patch just like it.

                I guess it might be neat
to own just one square foot of dirt: Earth's surface
to core, that's twenty million cubic feet!
In Virgil's Rome, a landless man, poor duffer,
was worth no more than his sister or his mother.

ROSEBUD, PUSTULE, BREAST

I have a virus I can't clear.
Papilla: Latin for rosebud, pustule, breast.
Look. I don't expect there to exist
an isomorphism between the list
of words and list of God-created things. I just
expected better than this.
Virus: Latin for poison, slime.
It's simmered inside me since my last
partner minus one. A long time.
Cervix: Latin for neck. This one implies
my womb is a decapitated thing
hung by its heels from a pair of steel rings.
Mine's a high-risk strain,
meaning more likely to cause cancer. *Cancer*
means crab. *Vaccine* means cow.
I was offered the vaccine once, years ago now,
but my insurance wouldn't pay for it,
so I turned it down. My insurance wouldn't pay
because some people don't believe
in vaccines, or in facts, or in sex, or in death.
I'd pay thousands for it now.
My headless bird without feathers! *Colposcopy*
means pain. High-risk strain. I expected better.

I, CASIMIR ŻORAWSKI, A MATHEMATICIAN OF POLAND,

met Manya on spring break in '86.
In studying more advanced arithmetics,

"Maria" was her birth name; "Manya" stuck
the most important law is one that took

because it had a gentler sound. She was
millennia to put in words because

my baby brother's nanny: blond, smoke-eyed.
it seems so obvious, one wonders why

it need be said at all. It states that if
Two teens in love, we itched to wed for life,

you have some pickle jars, you can select
but Dad forbade it, saying, "I expect

one pickle from each jar. The Axiom
that no-name slut will end up in a slum."

of Choice, it's called: the basis of set theory.
She's married now; her married name is Curie.

¡ALMAS HERMANAS MÍAS!

for Delmira Agustini, on the centennial of her death

Delmira is dead.
Red as a geranium
her blood-soaked head.

Two termites of lead
bored through her cranium
and now she's dead.

She shared her bed
with Enrique, a maniac
who turned her head.

They were one month wed
when her born Italian
wits woke: *You're dead*

to me, Quique, she said
and left. This millennium's
blue-eyed figurehead,

she lived, wrote, without dread.
Now she's gone subterranean,
hauled anchor, is dead.

Sisters, keep a wise head.

DEEP MEN

deep
                    men
            carry
            the risk of
        setting
        a   lo / bar.
deep   m-
en   are strong
  with burden of white
        intensities.
        pathologic,
                clearly high.
                almost in-
variably
                sensitive,
                patient
                men   who
        will not   play,
certainly supportive in the appropriate
setting.
MR.
Comb,   we can
summarize: between the
                    decline
and
        further decline,
        the average
        did not   control
me.
                        might i
                suggest i
                decline
        to be
                treat-

ed
as
hemorrhage?
i   posit   complication.
                    agnostic, i
        search
    his
    valence;
no   true
fact
                    i find.

Source for this erasure: Sven Haller, et al. "Cerebral Microbleeds: Imaging and Clinical Significance." *Radiology* 287, no. 1 (2018):16, https://doi.org/10.1148/radiol.2018170803.

NOVEMBER

November is a mammal, smoke-gray, meek.
Its lumbering body uses weighty flippers
to paddle, making short-lived silver streaks
in the surface of the bay where it's immersed.

It loves the brackish waters of year's end,
where black-green tufts of daydreams toss and seethe,
the fodder that it munches till it's fattened
and farts its way up toward the sun to breathe.

At times, its blimp-like bulk, incautious, crashes
into our worries, our hurry to complete
our home-improvement plans before the fractious
first snow, our human habit to mistreat

each other, our campaign ads, our work stress.
It wears those scars from one year to the next.

MANIA

Your trapezoidal face, like Townes Van Zandt's,
makes my pulse race more than the razzmatazz
of Times Square, makes my p- and t-waves dance
more than a jailbreak out of Alcatraz.
Look how my EKG goes crazy now;
look how my EEG goes mad, synapses
zapping and zigzagging everywhere—wow!
I'm wakeful as a raft about to capsize
but oh-so-happy. Cap my trazodone,
please. Zip up my zapatas, please. Let's seize
tonight's flight to Tasmania's time zone.
When strapped onto the TNT trapeze
of love, we'll tell our pals, "Ta-ta! That's that!"
and tap-dance off into the rat-a-tat.

I SING: HOLY

HOMEMADE ECLIPSE GLASSES

My friend Meshulum, medical
man, made a beeline through the catacombs
to the greenhouse of white vines where mammograms
are made,

took a surplus sheet
of film, and exposed it
until only one in a thousand
rays of sun would penetrate
that black square.

A MacGyvered monocle. This
shielded his retinas from being roasted
by the total eclipse. Kids,
don't try this on your home planet.

He siphoned supplies
earmarked for breasts,
repurposing them for eyes. On behalf of all
brassiere wearers, I declare
his deed

consecrated, blessed.
In the name of the milk glands
molded to my own chest,
I sing: holy

is the man
who dowsed a darkness
meant to minister to softness
and, Icarus-like,
wore it to whicker at the sun.

A CULTURAL ARTIFACT

Guy Goodrich posts on Facebook, nine a.m.:
"Bam-Bam, my cat, is now in kidney failure."
"Waht dredful news!" Jean Leathers posts at ten.
"Hope Bam feels better," Tim posts minutes later.

Sam Hamm, at noon, posts, "What is kidney failure?"
At half past noon, Michelle posts, "[Frowny face.]"
"Hope Bam gets better!!!!!!!!!!!" Kim posts seconds later.
At one, Wayne posts, "Stay strong, man, with God's grace."

Then: "I just put Bam down," Guy posts. "[Sad face.]"
"So sorry for your loss," Tim posts at two.
"So very sorry, Guy. Stay strong," posts Grace.
Ross T., at four, posts, "Sending vibes at you."

"So sorry for your loss!!!!!!!!!!!" Kim posts. "Me, too,"
comments Kim's mom. "oh no," posts Lily Deere.
Ross C.: "I know Bam meant the world to you."
Val Schubbs posts, "Always glad to lend an ear . . ."

At six, Quinn posts, "Hope Bam mends soon, my dear."
Guy Goodrich: "See above, Quinn. Bam is dead."
Quinn: "Oops! My bad! *tomato-colored ears*
That's what comes of not reading the whole thread."

HOW WE MET

I want to confess everything
about the cow behind the fence

at whose sight I blurted "Horse!"
so that I then had to pretend

it was a horse I saw. What fibs we tell
to gloss over the fact

God's fly is always down.
I looked the other way

to spare Him unease;
that's how I met your blue eyes

across the cocktail lounge. It's how I met
everyone I've ever met.

TỊNH ĐỘ TÔNG

We Buddhists often speak of a "Pure Land,"
where a man swathed in jackfruit cloth awaits us,
lotus blossoms wide-mouthed in his hands.

*

The Hebrew Bible says a "Promised Land,"
a milk-and-honey-sticky place, awaits us.
Buddhists, though, believe in a Pure Land,
where peacocks sail aloft and never land
and where a man with sun-red heart awaits us,
lotus blossoms spilling from his hands.

*

Just as the late sun tints west-lying land,
our brows flush pink with hopes for what awaits us
in that westmost country, the Pure Land.

*

Six-pointed stars denote the Jewish land;
they stand, too, for the lotus that awaits us,
whose musky anthers scent the Buddha's hands.

*

If we could somehow see our flawed homeland
as equal to the heaven that awaits us,
we'd be at once transported to that Land—
its lotuses would leap into our hands.

WAKING FROM ANESTHESIA

Waking from anesthesia
    after the operation
        that proved beyond all doubt
            his cancer had recurred,
   my nineteen-year-old patient,
only son of a preacher,
          turned to me and slurred,
       "There's something I wanna shout,"

and when I asked him, "What?"
    he smiled just like a doll
        (above his plump brown cheeks
           his eyes were glassy from
    the fading propofol)
and mumbled, mouth half-shut,
          "I'm sexy as they come"—
    just the sort of oblique

nonsense all drugged folks blurt
    and then forget they've blurted
        one minute later. Still,
          I hope that when he wakes
   in the afterlife charted
        out by his faith, his aches
    will be gone and he'll feel
like the sexiest man on earth.

A LIFE

1

I visit Marjorie in her hospital room.
A mustached man with an intense stare hovers
beside her bed—Who is he? Her new lover?
I wait for Marge to introduce the gloom-
eyed stranger, but she acts like she can't see
him, though he's standing just one foot away,
his gaze immovably fixed on her face.
At last, unstrung by curiosity,
I hiss, "Who is he?" Flatly, she explains:
"That's Bo, the nursing aide assigned to stalk
my every piddling movement, round the clock,
so that I don't try suicide again."

2

A picture, black-and-white, of Marjorie
appeared in Nassau County's *Daily Times*
the tenth of January, '59:
the caption calls her "Miss," describes how she
played bridesmaid in a friend's society wedding
in "pale pink bell-shaped skirt," headpiece of "tulle."
You could describe her face as beautiful
in that small grainy photograph. The setting's
a rural churchyard, thick with hardy gingkoes.
She stands amid a clutch of other belles
as dewy as she is, wide eyes enspelled
like a bird that's flown into a picture window.

AGAINST EMPIRICISM

True, no one can prove
the sun will rise tomorrow.
Still, I know for sure
Miss Dunne of Teterboro

will rise at five and dress
herself with no one's aid,
then, leaning on the oak
cane she inherited

when her twin brother died
four years ago (she still
gets teary at the thought),
apply her steadfast will

to descend the thirty steps
from apartment down to street,
give dollar bills and candy
to neighbors' kids she meets,

and keep all her appointments
with punctuality
the way her father taught her
as a girl in Tennessee,

so, no matter what
Hume says in his *Enquiry*,
in a way it's certain
the sun will rise a priori.

PICKY PICKY

I don't want the whole sandwich,
just the cucumbers and mayo.
I don't want to have sex,
just the part that feels transcendent.
I don't want to read your novel,
just the parts that are about me.
I don't want to watch *It's a Wonderful Life*,
just the ending, over and over.
I don't want to listen to the Killers station on Pandora,
just the Killers, and just the songs I like.
I don't want to learn guitar,
just enough to make you lick your lips.
I don't want to master Latin,
just enough to dig Propertius.
I don't want an Instant Pot,
just the meals that someone's made in one.
I don't want daylight savings time,
just the hour we gain for free.
I don't want all-wheel drive,
just the guarantee of safety.
I don't want sriracha hot sauce,
just for the sriracha inventor to prosper.
I don't want an Instant Pot,
just for the Instant Pot inventor to prosper.
I don't want to write a poem,
just the words between the rhyme words.
I don't want to write a poem,
just the rhyme words, nothing else.

STANDING BETWEEN MY PARENTS AT MANATEE LAGOON

My sister took this photo, and I like,
well, everything about it:

                  its mostly cool
blue palette, challenged here and there by spiky
aneurysmal daubs of red;

                  the cruel
sharpness with which noon light outlines our faces
so that our proud straight selves resemble three
rock monuments;

                the wide and even spaces
that separate us, gaps where, quietly,
with creeping certainty, the sea intrudes;

the invisibility of the manatees,
which you must take on faith, for all that you'd
prefer to see hard proof of their brown creased
skins simmering in the shallows and not rely
on trust,

          my false friend;
                  the sunless, sun-hot sky.

WE ARE ALL AT LEAST 50 PERCENT WATER

A "snowmaking whale" is a man-made pile of snow produced
by pressurized snow cannons at a ski resort.

In my last life I was a humpback whale,
wide-set eyes glowering sidelong from
skin folds near my armpits. My grim
fluted lower lip, pocked with drunkard's Braille,

jabbed up and outward like a shelf of shale,
continuing the drab atonal hymn
engraved in droning curves along my scummed
underbelly, stretching to my tail.

My death lacked drama: a mere overflow
of days across a sandbar. I'm a snow
whale now, no eyes, no lip, just sparkling hump,

and when the wind that peppers skiers' eyes
lets rip at me, big scoops of me arise,
unsew themselves from me, and leave no stump.

ACKNOWLEDGMENTS

Angle: "The Twelve Dancing Princesses"

Baltimore Review: "Standing between My Parents at Manatee Lagoon"

Carolina Quarterly: "Please Don't Tell Me How the Story Ends"

Cherry Tree: "Rosebud, Pustule, Breast"

Cha: An Asian Literary Journal: "The Ballad of Great-Uncle Chi"

Cider Press Review: "How I Know Implicit Bias Exists"

Cincinnati Review: "Capgras/Seagrass," "The Reader"

Copper Nickel: "Private Rituals"

Denver Quarterly: "A Cultural Artifact," "A Life," "What the Ancient Greek Sailors Knew"

Ekphrastic Review: "*Patti Smith*, 1976," "Posture," "*Venus Frigida*"

The Examined Life Journal: "Waking from Anesthesia"

The Fourth River: "Sibling Rivalry"

Glass: A Journal of Poetry: "Women Who Conjure Owls"

The Hollins Critic: "Tịnh Độ Tông"

I-70 Review: "To John Ashbery"

Juked: "deep men"

Light: "A Very Asian Variation"

LIT: "Bird"

Literary Matters: "Purses"

Little Patuxent Review: "New York Living"

Mezzo Cammin: "Against Empiricism," "What Do You Want to Be When You Grow Up?"

Michigan Quarterly Review: "Homemade Eclipse Glasses"

Nasty Women Poets (Lost Horse Press): "On the Lesser-Known Uses of Meat Tenderizer"

New Verse News: "November," "Sirenian Sermon," "To a Physician Killed by Gun Violence"

Pleiades: "Quixotic"

Poet Lore: "Picky Picky"

Poetry by the Sea (2019 Sonnet Competition Winner): "Mania"

Potomac Review: "A Failed Georgic"

Rise Up Review: "Bird-Watching in the Aftermath"

Rosebud: "We Are All at Least 50 Percent Water"

Salt Hill: "Echoes"

Sixth Finch: "Neurology Ward Sketchbook"

SWWIM: "Golden Shovel in the Voice of Margot Begemann"

Tar River Poetry: "*Deipnosophistae*"

Thrush Poetry Journal: "¡Almas Hermanas Mías!"

Tinderbox Poetry Journal: "Woman behind the Lens"

Poems in the Aftermath (Indolent Books): "The Morning after the Election"

Rattle Poets Respond feature: "Gusanoz"

Virga: "Dispatch from Hanover, New Hampshire"

Waccamaw: "I, Casimir Żorawski, a Mathematician of Poland"

Washington Square Review: "How We Met"

West Branch: "The Origami Master Breakfasts with His New Apprentice"